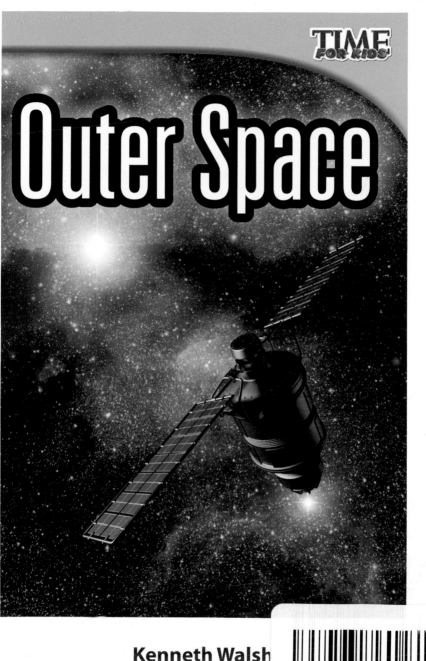

Outer Space

TIME FOR KIDS

Kenneth Walsh

Consultant

Timothy Rasinski, Ph.D.
Kent State University

Publishing Credits

Dona Herweck Rice, *Editor-in-Chief*
Robin Erickson, *Production Director*
Lee Aucoin, *Creative Director*
Conni Medina, M.A.Ed., *Editorial Director*
Jamey Acosta, *Editor*
Stephanie Reid, *Photo Editor*
Rachelle Cracchiolo, M.S.Ed., *Publisher*

Based on writing from *TIME For Kids*.

TIME For Kids and the *TIME For Kids* logo are registered trademarks of TIME Inc. Used under license.

Teacher Created Materials

5301 Oceanus Drive
Huntington Beach, CA 92649-1030
http://www.tcmpub.com

ISBN 978-1-4333-3632-4

© 2012 Teacher Created Materials, Inc.
Made in China
Nordica.072017.CA21700824

Table of Contents

Twinkle, Twinkle

Twinkle, twinkle little **star**, do you know just where you are?

Outer Space

If you are a star, you are somewhere in **outer space**. What is outer space? Is it everything far into the sky?

Our Universe

Universe is a word for everything in space, including Earth.

Yes, outer space is the huge space that holds everything there is beyond Earth, from the smallest speck to the largest **galaxy**.

Outer space is huge. It is so big that it has not stopped growing! We cannot reach the edge of space because the ends keep growing outward.

Imagine if you never stopped growing!

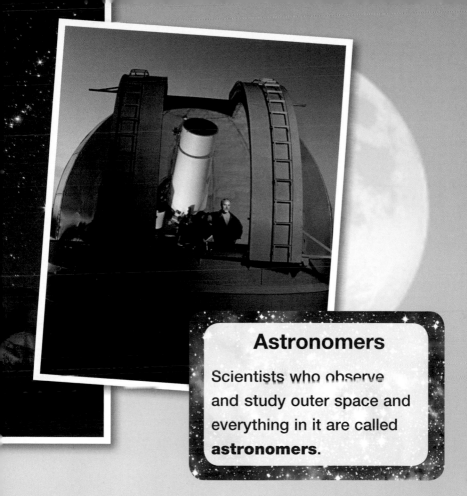

Astronomers

Scientists who observe and study outer space and everything in it are called **astronomers**.

When we think of outer space, we usually think of everything far out in the sky and beyond. We think of galaxies, stars, and **comets**. We think of **planets** and the sun. All of these things are part of outer space.

Galaxies

Galaxies are made of groups of stars, gas, and dust that are held together by **gravity**.

There are billions of galaxies in outer space. Earth is part of the **Milky Way Galaxy**.

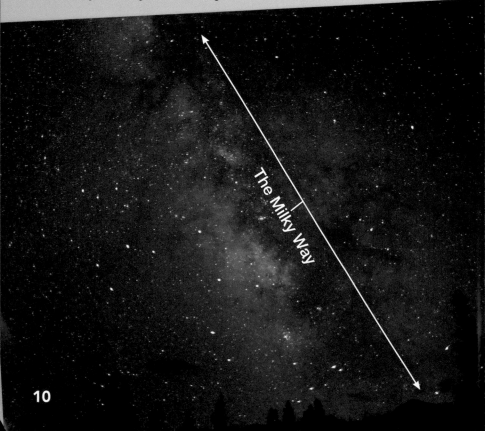

The Milky Way

Spitzer Space Telescope

How do we learn about outer space? One way is to look through powerful telescopes, like the Spitzer Space Telescope. The Spitzer is a satellite orbiting in space and taking pictures for us. Here is one of the photos it took.

Millions and Billions

A **million** is 1,000,000. A **billion** is 1,000,000,000. There are millions of stars in some galaxies and billions of stars in others. There are more than 100 billion stars in the Milky Way. It would take 3,000 years to count them!

Earth

sun

The Milky Way

Why is our galaxy called the Milky Way? Ancient Greeks thought it looked like a road made of milk. In fact, our word *galaxy* comes from *gala*, the Greek word for milk.

The Milky Way looks like a giant blue pinwheel with a yellow center. The oldest stars are in the center. Younger stars are in the pinwheel arms. Our sun and planet Earth are there.

The Milky Way spins like a pinwheel, too. All the stars spin fast around the center.

Stars

Outer space is filled with stars, and new stars are forming all the time.

Stars are big balls of gas that give off heat and light. Young stars are bright blue. Older stars are yellow, orange, and red. Stars change slowly over time. They can live for billions of years!

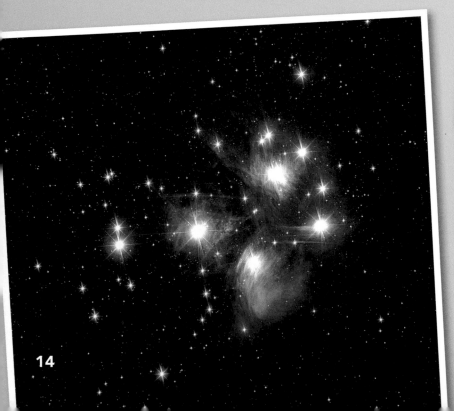

black hole

Black Holes

When gravity makes a very large star collapse into itself, we call it a black hole. Black holes have strong gravity. Anything that is close will get pulled into it and never get out. Even light cannot escape.

It may look as
though all the stars
are close together in
space, but they are
not. There is so much
space that it takes
light 100,000 years
just to travel across
the Milky Way galaxy.
So, each star has
plenty of room.

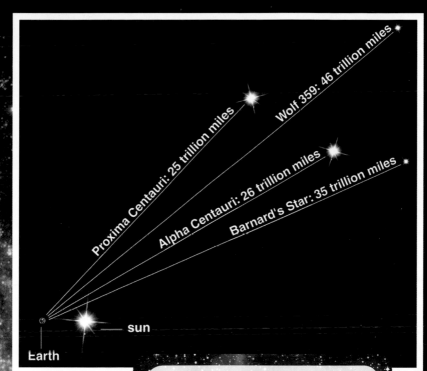

Proxima Centauri: 25 trillion miles
Wolf 359: 46 trillion miles
Alpha Centauri: 26 trillion miles
Barnard's Star: 35 trillion miles
sun
Earth

Star Distances

Our sun is the closest star to Earth. It is 93 million miles away. This graph shows the stars closest to Earth.

The Sun

Did you know that our sun is a bright, yellow star? It gives us light and warmth.

Among many other stars, the sun spins in the Milky Way. It moves 140 miles each second! How fast is that? The fastest cars only move one tiny part of a mile each second.

A Speeding Bullet

Our sun moves 300 times faster
than a speeding bullet! Earth is
moving fast around the sun, too,
but we do not feel it. It is like
when you are in a car driving at
a fast speed. Although the car is
moving quickly, inside the car it
may feel as if you are not moving
at all.

Asteroids, Comets, and Meteors

comet

asteroids

Asteroids are oddly shaped rocks or piles of gravel. They orbit the sun like planets do.

Millions of asteroids orbit together in the asteroid belt between Mars and Jupiter. Others orbit closer to Earth and sometimes smash into it.

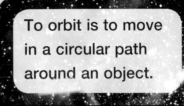

To orbit is to move in a circular path around an object.

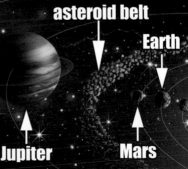

asteroid belt

Earth

Jupiter

Mars

Comets look like bright balls with long tails. They are made of frozen gases and dust. When a comet nears the sun, its outer layers become a vapor tail.

A comet's tail is millions and millions of miles long!

Vapor

Vapor is the gas form of something, instead of its liquid or solid state. Vapor can be created because of heat.

Meteors are stones that fall from space toward Earth. Most of the time, they are parts of comets or asteroids. They usually burn up on their way to Earth. If they reach Earth, we call them **meteorites**.

Who Knew?

2,500 years ago, a Greek man named Anaxagoras (an-ak-SAG-er-uhs) found a rock that he believed came from the sky instead of Earth. He was the first person to make that discovery.

Planets

Planets are large bodies in space that orbit a star. They have no light of their own. They get light from the star.

Other Planets

Astronomers saw planets that orbit stars other than our sun for the first time in 1991. They used special telescopes to see them.

MERCURY
VENUS
EARTH
MARS
JUPITER
SATURN
URANUS
NEPTUNE
PLUTO

Is Pluto a Planet?

Pluto was once considered the ninth planet in our solar system. It has been reclassified as a dwarf planet.

Earth is one of eight planets orbiting our sun. But there are more planets in outer space. They are too far away for us to visit now. We do not know as much about them as we might if we could visit them.

People and Outer Space

People have changed space by sending things into it. We have sent **satellites** and space stations into orbit. We have flown rockets to the moon. We have even sent probes into deep, deep space to take pictures of things.

Satellites are objects in space that orbit other larger objects.

Long ago, people never imagined traveling into space, but today we can. Who knows how far we will go in the future! Maybe one day we will fly out of our solar system. Maybe we will travel to other galaxies.

Glossary

asteroids—the small, rocky, planet-like bodies that orbit the sun

astronomer—a scientist who observe and study outer space and everything in it

billion—1,000,000,000

comets—the balls of frozen gas and dust with long vapor tails that move through space

galaxy—the groups of stars, gas, and dust that are held together by gravity

gravity—a natural force that pulls objects toward each other

meteorites—the meteors that strike Earth

meteors—the stones that fall from space toward Earth

million—1,000,000

Milky Way Galaxy—Earth's galaxy

outer space—the space beyond Earth from the smallest speck to the largest galaxy

planets—the large bodies in space that orbit a star

satellites—the objects in space that orbit another larger object

star—a big ball of gas that gives off heat and light

universe—everything in space, including Earth